DOG BITE PREVENTION

Created by
M. Peggy A. Rew
All Rights Reserved

Printings:
2nd Edition: 1st – July 2020,
1st Edition: 6th – 2018, 5th – May 2016, 4th – December 2014,
3rd – June 2014, 2nd – September 2013, 1st – October 2012

Published by
Graphospasm Kollabrative, LLC dba RewCrew Collaborations
Sparks, Nevada www.rewcrew.com

Printing by
Abbott's Printing, Inc., Yakima, WA www.abbottsprinting.com

Dogs are very smart creatures...just like you!

Let's learn how dogs use all their senses and non-verbal body language to communicate with us!

Sight: Eyes see everything
Hearing: Ears are vital for safety and hear things humans can't
Taste: Tongues help dogs recognize people/food & sweat
Smell: Noses can detect food, sickness, and fear
Touch, Body Language & Barking:
Paws, tails, belly rubs and barking tell all kinds of stories about dogs

If we can learn what dogs are trying to tell us,
we'll be able to enjoy each other's company without being scared
and can avoid accidental dog bites.

A DOG'S EYES

Dogs watch everything, so watch how they look as you approach them. Dogs can be playful, protective, grumpy, or scared.

Even if you can't see a dog's eyes, they can still see you.
Please be sure a dog knows you're walking towards them.
Even if you know the dog, call their name, whistle, or clap your hands.

Be gentle and cautious
if a dog is sight impaired.

Most dogs don't even
realize they are impaired,
but it's nice
to let them know
you're here.

**Don't be scared,
be prepared!**

Move slowly around unfamiliar dogs or
one may nip at you out of fear.

They can feel stranger-danger, too.

No matter how big or small, all dogs need
proper introductions...
even gentle giants or tiny yappers.

YOU don't have to be scared
 if you are prepared!

When you jump rope, kick balls, ride bikes and skateboards, dogs may want to follow and play.

Don't move too quickly! Stand still and talk to the dog until it can figure out which direction you are going. **Don't be scared!**

Be prepared!

If a dog follows and you feel scared, stop your bike, scooter, or skateboard. Keep your ride between you and the dog, but let it sniff you.

The dog may be lost or hungry or even protective if it doesn't recognize you. Just stand still. If you're walking, use your backpack as a barrier.

You can stand like a tree by raising your arms up like branches or just fold them across your chest.

Always give dogs a chance to sniff you.
If they are lost,
they may be just as scared as you.
Maybe you'll get lucky and make a new friend.

Dogs can hear things up close and far away
plus many noises can make them howl, moan and bark!

Take notice of how they tilt their heads and lift their ears to hear kids laughing, a ball bouncing, wind blowing, sirens and other loud noises.

Dog ears come in all shapes and sizes.
They can hear everything plus sounds humans cannot hear.

Loud disturbances and high pitch sounds can upset some dogs.
It may hurt their ears, so let them listen, howl and bark.
Noises like fireworks, screaming or sirens can change their mood.
Be gentle and loving and be prepared to take them home.
Give hugs and use fresh lavender on blankets and collars to calm them down.

Big dogs,

lit_le dogs,

big ears,

little ears.

Please don't tug on any dog's ears.
It can hurt and upset them and make them bite!

Dog ears shouldn't be tugged on. Some dogs don't like their heads or ears touched. So please always, always ask the owner before petting a dog.

Don't be scared, be prepared!

Many breeds of dogs can tell if you're happy, sad, scared, or tired.

Or do you feel like playing or cuddling?

Give them a chance to hear you and understand what you want to do.

Dog tongues are like another set of eyes.
They search for tasty things and sometimes you're tasty.

Be careful if you have food on or in your hands.
Don't be scared, be prepared!

When dogs smile, they can show their teeth or let their tongue hang out which can mean they are happy.

Sometimes it's hard to keep their tongue in their mouth.

Dogs might want to lick you because of something you ate
or if you smell like another dog.

If you have food in your hands, please do not hand it to a dog.
The dog might mistake one of your fingers for a treat.

Dogs use their tongues to sense their surroundings, too.
If you are walking your dogs, don't let them pick up garbage.
It could be bad for their tummies.

Tongues may slobber.
Tongues may surprise you and wipe a kiss across your face!
A dog's long tongue can look dangerous or scary, but remember,
tongues are particularly important for interacting with humans.

A DOG'S NOSE

Dog noses come in all shapes and sizes on dogs of all shapes and sizes.
Some dog noses make funny noises.
Bulldogs and Boxers make snorting sounds that may sound scary, but they just how they breathe. If they get overexcited, they can be real **noisy**!

Dachshunds sometime wheeze, sneeze, or choke like
an allergy attack when they get excited.

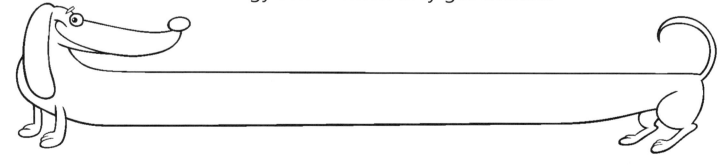

Talk to the owner about noises and you'll always be prepared.
Never having to be scared.

From far, faraway, dogs can smell flowers, food, fresh air, and smoke,
but they can also notice smells on you and stinky stuff on the street.
Again, don't let them pick up garbage.

Dogs use their noses to say Hi and get to know you.
Did you just eat something yummy? Were you playing with another dog?
Some dogs are smart enough to know if you are sick.
Noses are so important.

When dogs sniff you all over,
they're deciding if it's ok to be friends.

Take your time
to get to know each other,
so no one gets scared.

There are many types of dogs just like there are many different humans.

Since all dogs are different, they will greet you differently.
Always give dogs a chance to sniff you so you can be friends,
but remember not all want to be friends.

A Dog's Touch,
Body Language
And Barking

Dogs like to touch you sometimes with all parts of their body.
Always ask the owner if you can touch them back.
Being nice to dogs makes you a nice human. We can all be friends, without
fear, if we ask permission and respect boundaries.

Be prepared to have a friend for life!

Dogs touch with their noses, tongues, tails and by barking.

Barking is their way of talking. If one is barking, they can be happy to see you or maybe they sense a stranger near you or their yard or at their gate.

Be aware of your surroundings.

If you're playing or riding your bike, dogs usually want to be with you.

Before you start riding, know where all dogs are so everyone stays safe to avoid accidents and injuries to you or the dogs.

BOUNDARIES

If we respect other people's yards and boundaries, we all stay safe.

Everyone has boundaries in their life. Learning what boundaries are is especially important is you don't want to get bit accidently.
Your yard, your neighbors' yards (fenced or not), is a boundary.
Always ask permission before you cross someone's boundary or you could get bit. Be prepared!

Boundaries include a dog's house, kennel, bed, blanket, food dish, chew toy or bone, or even their leash.
Please <u>do not cross</u> these boundaries as some dogs might feel the need to be afraid or very protective.

Don't be scared, be prepared!

Entering a gated yard without permission, especially if you hear a dog barking behind the fence, can be dangerous for you and scary for the dog.

Any sign on the gate or fence means the homeowner is telling you to **STAY OUT**! **DO NOT** ever jump over someone's fence without permission.

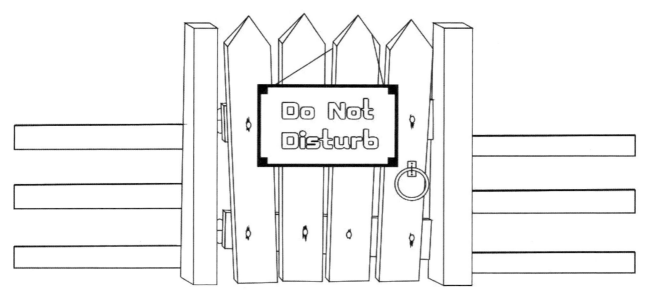

Ask your parents to call them or go to the front door and ask the neighbor to get whatever is over there. Trespassing on someone else's property is serious, so please respect your boundaries.

Dogs can be very protective of their yards and you do not want to upset them or get them in trouble for doing their job.

Working dogs come in all shapes and sizes.
Dogs get excited about their jobs and can be extremely focused.

Service or companion dogs aren't allowed to visit or play while *'on duty.'*
Be respectful of this essential job as
this is an important boundary you must not cross.
Their owner must remove their uniform and give you permission to touch.

Another boundary is a mother dog and her litter of pups. It is her job to protect the babies, so respect her space until she welcomes you to visit.

If you want to visit and pet the puppies, always ask the dog's owner first.
Never reach into a mama dog's bed and touch the puppies.
This will upset everyone causing unnecessary dog bites.
<u>Warning</u>: when you do pet the pups, watch out as some have sharp teeth.
They might nibble on your fingers.

It's always better to **be prepared**, so **no one is scared**
especially the mama dog and the puppies.

If a dog is sleeping, let them sleep. Sleeping is another boundary!
If you must wake them, call out their name, stomp your foot,
clap your hands, or whistle.
Some old dogs can't hear very well and you may scare them.
Give dogs a chance to wake and recognize you.

Try not to startle a dog is they are sleeping even if you know them.
Dogs can have bad dreams or wake up grumpy just like you!
Beware of small ones who may bark a bit.
They can be afraid of being stepped on, so just might nip at you.

If a dog decides it wants to be your friend,
you may just get to shake paws or give a belly rub.

Be gentle and affectionate, so no nipping occurs.

Being prepared around dogs makes it less scary for all.

You may love dogs and dogs may love you, but be incredibly careful not to kiss them on or near their face particularly if you and the dog are strangers.

Always ask the human owner before reaching for or petting a dog.

You've learned a lot about dogs.
So many types of dogs and so many ways for them to talk to us.
Now you can help all dogs communicate better with humans by understanding how they use their senses and body language.

Together, let's be a <u>voice for the voiceless</u> by respecting all boundaries and asking permission to give them some love and attention.

Don't be scared, just be prepared!!!